ALL ABOUT HER

Treasured Memories

My diary for remembering & healing

Juli M Halifax

Printed in the United States of America

First Edition, Treasured Memories (all about her version), a diary for remembering and healing 2016.

ISBN 978-0692714867 (soft cover
Title: Treasured Memories, (all about her version) a diary for remembering and healing. Category: 1. Children; grieving, grief, mourning, loss 2. Children's journals; diary, journaling, storytelling

For permission requests and bulk book ordering, write to the author at the address below:
Juli M. Halifax
100 S Belcher Rd, #7414
Clearwater, FL 33758
www.julihalifax.com
hello@julihalifax.com

This diary is dedicated to all the children who have
been faced with the heartbreak of losing a loved one.

To my brother Jamie, you are so sorely missed. This creation has
helped me to deal with the severe pain of losing you.

Uncle Lorenzo Jr., no words or stories could ever adequately
convey how special you were to so many who knew and loved you.
Thank you for always being there, for your generosity and your sarcasm.

Acknowledgements

To my nephew who inspired me to write this journal.
My niece, I apologize for not giving you one of these in
the early days. I took for granted that you were okay because
you still had your mother to hold and guide you.
My sister, brother and mother who also lost a chunk of
their hearts that will never be filled. My husband who has
encouraged me to make time to share this idea with others
and who supports me in my endeavors. My friend Dana
and mother-in-law for all the hours taking care of Gavin.
My dearest friends Dana, Maria, Teresa, AnnMarie and
Jessica for your support and valued input and feedback.

Thank you to Pinellas County Libraries and staff for the countless
hours of use of their computers and private rooms.

Treasured Memories

Preface

The reason...

This memory journal was created out of my own experience in unexpectedly losing my beloved brother due to a tragic accident.

At the time of his death, he was only 33 years old, leaving behind two young children. At age 10, his son came to live with my husband and me. We did not know how long he would be with us and at that time, I was spiraling into a depression. My nephew and I were not *that* close when he became a part of our household. However, I loved him dearly... after all, not only was he my nephew, he was 50% of what I had left of my brother, he was his namesake and he was a miniature version of him. Right down to his sneeze!

Although our relationship was "new", we had something in common – we were both in need of healing and we both wanted to hang onto my brother for as long as possible. I did not want him to forget anything at all. Each night, at bedtime, he would ask me to tell him stories about my brother. Night after night, I would recall a memory or two and tell him stories about his dad. Sometimes, I would ask him to share with me some of the things he loved, missed and experienced with his dad. It was my way of helping him vent, and unbeknownst to me, it turned out that I learned more about my brother that I hadn't known.

It was during these fragile first months, that I had the idea to create a journal for him to store his memories – through the eyes and heart of a child... I wanted him to have a safe, private place to share his feelings whenever he felt he needed to, on his own time, with or without my or anyone else's help.

I hope that this memory journal will help your child or the child you are gifting it to as much, if not more than it helped my nephew and me. I hope this will aide in the journey of healing.

From my heart to yours,

Juli H.

Treasured Memories,

A diary for remembering and healing

My name is _____ and I am _____ years old.

My _____ are/is going to help me write down memories I have and help me to understand why this has happened.

I will write in this diary whenever I want to. Sometimes, I may want to write down something happy and sometimes, it may be something sad. There might be days when I may want to just look through this diary and not write down anything at all. I can look at the pictures and think happy thoughts about our times together.

Even though she is not here in person for me to talk to or spend time with the way we did before she left, I will know that her spirit is with me all the time. Our memories are mine to keep forever, and this diary will help keep them close to my heart.

My aching heart will begin to feel better...

Slowly...

Starting... now ☺

"You are always with me although I cannot see you"

Treasured Memories was created for you.
This is your diary to fill with all the special memories you
have or memories that others have shared with you about
the person you lost, miss and will love always and forever.

Inside, you will find pages to fill with special things about the
person you lost, areas for drawing, pasting pictures and more.

10 IMPORTANT RULES

(For the owner of this diary and the grown up helping to write it)

1. There are no rules on how to fill this out.
2. There are no rules on how often you should write in here.
3. Anything you write in here is PRIVATE, unless you want someone else to read it.
4. You can write in this diary anytime you want to.
5. You will never be too young or too old to write in here.
6. You can keep this diary forever and ever!
7. You can use a pencil or pen, crayons or markers.
8. Cutting pictures out and taping or gluing them in here would be great.
9. If there is a page where you wrote something that you don't feel like seeing every time you are using your diary, tape a piece of paper over it or fold the page over. (Doing this will help you avoid seeing those thoughts or feelings until you are ready to see them again.)
10. It is OK to cry and, it is OK to laugh when you feel ready.

About her

I am writing about my _____.

Her name was _____ and she was _____ years old

when she passed away.

She had _____ hair and _____ eyes.

About her

Some of her hobbies were _____

_____

_____

_____

She was a _____ person; I think this because she

_____

_____

_____

_____

My favorite story about her told to me by _____ is

_____

_____

_____

_____

_____

_____

Farewell thoughts

She is no longer with our family because _____

_____

_____

_____

Something that I said to her before she left was _____

_____

_____

_____

_____

Something that I said wanted to say before she left was _____

_____

_____

_____

_____

For her celebration of her life memorial/funeral, our family

_____

_____

_____

_____

_____

Treasured Memories

Farewell thoughts

On that day, I felt like _____

_____

_____

_____

_____

_____

_____

_____

_____

I wanted to say _____

_____

_____

_____

_____

_____

_____

_____

_____

_____

Farewell thoughts

I want her to know that _____

_____

_____

_____

_____

_____

_____

_____

In her memory, I will _____

_____

_____

_____

_____

_____

_____

_____

_____

_____

I feel like writing...   *Today is* _____

_____

_____

_____

_____

_____

_____

_____

_____

_____

_____

_____

_____

_____

_____

_____

_____

_____

_____

I feel like writing...   *Today is* _____

_____

_____

_____

_____

_____

_____

_____

_____

_____

_____

_____

_____

_____

_____

_____

_____

_____

_____

_____

I feel like writing...   *Today is* _____

_____

_____

_____

_____

_____

_____

_____

_____

_____

_____

_____

_____

_____

_____

_____

_____

_____

_____

_____

_____

I feel like writing...   *Today is* _____

_____

_____

_____

_____

_____

_____

_____

_____

_____

_____

_____

_____

_____

_____

_____

_____

_____

_____

I feel like writing...   *Today is* _____

_____

_____

_____

_____

_____

_____

_____

_____

_____

_____

_____

_____

_____

_____

_____

_____

_____

_____

_____

I feel like drawing...   Today is _____

I feel like drawing...   *Today is _____*

ABOUT US

This is one of my favorite pictures of us together

In this picture, we were at _____

_____

_____

This is one of my favorite pictures because _____

_____

_____

_____

On that day, I remember _____

_____

_____

_____

ABOUT US

I had the most fun with her when we _____

_____

_____

_____

_____

_____

_____

_____

_____

More fun memories or things I would have liked to do with her

_____

_____

_____

_____

_____

_____

_____

_____

_____

ABOUT US

This is what I miss most _____

_____

_____

_____

_____

_____

When we spent time together, she used to_____

_____

_____

_____

_____

_____

She taught me how to _____

_____

_____

_____

_____

_____

ABOUT US

Her favorite foods were

My favorite foods are

Her favorite color _____ and favorite number _____

My favorite color _____ and favorite number _____

This spot is for a drawing or thoughts

ABOUT US

These are some of the books we read together:

➤ _____

➤ _____

➤ _____

➤ _____

These are some of the movies we watched together:

➤ _____

➤ _____

➤ _____

➤ _____

These were our favorite songs **or** these songs remind me of

her:

➤ _____

➤ _____

➤ _____

➤ _____

Other things we did together or wish we had done:

➤ _____

➤ _____

➤ _____

➤ _____

OUR BIRTHDAYS

Her birthday was _____

Her favorite cake flavor was _____

She liked to _____ on her birthday

My birthday is _____

My favorite cake flavor is _____

I like to _____ on my birthday

My favorite birthday memories with her are:

_____

_____

_____

My favorite gift from her was: _____

_____

Write down your thoughts or draw a picture in the space

Treasured Memories

OUR FAMILY

Some of my favorite memories together as a family are _____

_____

_____

_____

_____

_____

This memory shared by _____

_____

_____

_____

_____

This memory shared by _____

_____

_____

_____

_____

_____

OUR FAMILY

My memory or memory shared by _____

_____

_____

_____

_____

_____

This memory shared by _____

_____

_____

_____

_____

_____

This memory shared by _____

_____

_____

_____

_____

_____

_____

OUR FAMILY

These are some of the places we went together:

- ➤ _____
- ➤ _____
- ➤ _____
- ➤ _____
- ➤ _____
- ➤ _____
- ➤ _____
- ➤ _____

DRAWING WHAT'S ON MY MIND

OUR FAMILY PHOTOS

Add your favorite pictures here

Treasured Memories

OUR FAMILY PHOTOS

Add your favorite pictures here

Treasured Memories

OUR FAMILY PHOTOS

Add your favorite pictures here

Treasured Memories

HOLIDAYS

On holidays, we: _____

_____

_____

_____

_____

In our family, we celebrate these holidays:

➢ _____

➢ _____

➢ _____

➢ _____

➢ _____

One of my favorite holiday memories that I have with her is

_____

_____

_____

I will miss _____

_____

_____

_____

_____

_____

HOLIDAY PHOTOS

Add your favorite pictures here

Treasured Memories

HOLIDAY PHOTOS

Add your favorite pictures here

Treasured Memories

HOLIDAY DRAWINGS OR CLIPPINGS

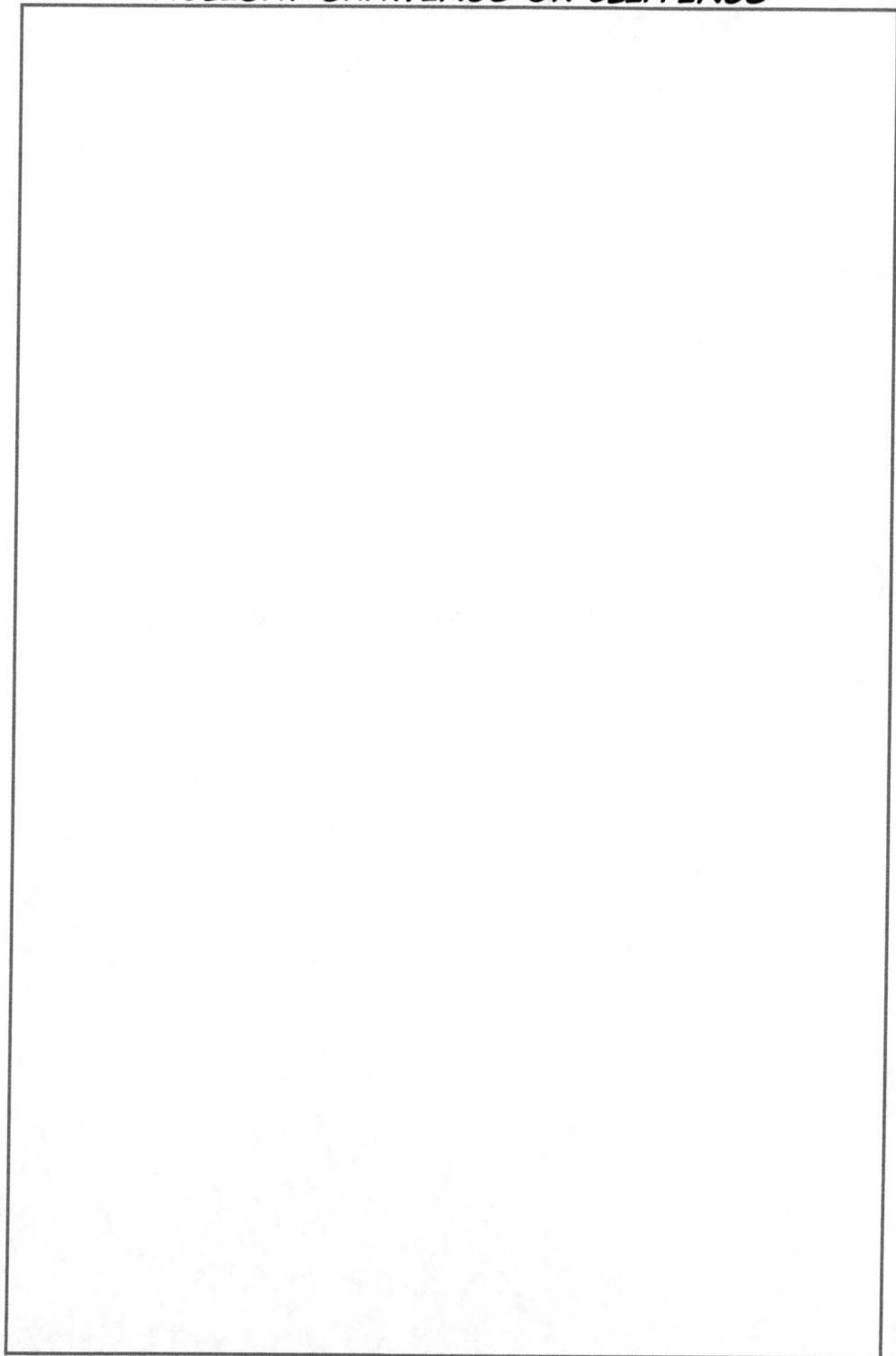

Treasured Memories

FEELINGS

There are different feelings you may experience. Your feelings can change from one day to the next. One day, you may feel sad and on another day, you may feel angry. There are days when you might feel happy – and that is very normal! She would not want you to be sad forever. She would want you to begin to feel better and enjoy your life. Share your feelings in this diary or talk about your feelings with someone who you feel most comfortable sharing with.

Sometimes, your sad feelings may sneak up on you when you least expect it. When I was sad from my loss, I would feel fine one minute, and then all of a sudden, I'd start to cry. It is 100% okay to feel this way! Little by little, these moments will come less often and you will begin to get used to her not being here in the same way she was before. You will always miss her and no one will ever take her place, but remember – she loved you and she would want you to be happy. How long it takes is up to you and your heart. There is no time limit or schedule, this is different for everyone. Please don't feel embarrassed or ashamed for any emotion you feel. The way you feel is normal and you have every right to feel the way you do.

Here are some feelings you may experience:

POSITIVE FEELINGS

HAPPY	LOVED	HOPEFUL	THANKFUL
PLAYFUL	HELPFUL	EXCITED	PEACEFUL

NEGATIVE FEELINGS

SAD	MAD	ANGRY	LONELY	CONFUSED
DENIAL	MEAN	GRUMPY	HOPELESS	BORED

OTHER EMOTIONS

Draw your happy feelings

Draw your sad feelings

How I feel at this moment _____

_____

_____

RIGHT NOW, I FEEL

Today is _____

_____

_____

_____

_____

_____

_____

_____

_____

_____

_____

_____

_____

_____

_____

_____

_____

_____

_____

_____

_____

RIGHT NOW, I FEEL   Today is _____

_____

_____

_____

_____

_____

_____

_____

_____

_____

_____

_____

_____

_____

_____

_____

_____

_____

RIGHT NOW, I FEEL　　　*Today is* _____

_____

_____

_____

_____

_____

_____

_____

_____

_____

_____

_____

_____

_____

_____

_____

_____

_____

_____

_____

RIGHT NOW, I FEEL   *Today is* _____

_____

_____

_____

_____

_____

_____

_____

_____

_____

_____

_____

_____

_____

_____

_____

_____

_____

_____

_____

_____

Treasured Memories

RIGHT NOW, I FEEL   *Today is* _____

_____

_____

_____

_____

_____

_____

_____

_____

_____

_____

_____

_____

_____

_____

_____

_____

_____

_____

_____

_____

Treasured Memories

I FEEL LIKE DRAWING   Today is _____

I FEEL LIKE DRAWING   Today is _____

I FEEL LIKE DRAWING   Today is _____

I FEEL LIKE DRAWING   *Today is* _____

THIS IS WHAT A _GOOD DAY_ LOOKS & FEELS LIKE

Today is _____

THIS IS WHAT A <u>BAD DAY</u> LOOKS & FEELS LIKE

Today is _____

IF I COULD CHANGE ANYTHING, IT WOULD BE...

_____

_____

_____

_____

_____

_____

_____

_____

_____

_____

_____

_____

_____

_____

_____

_____

_____

_____

_____

IF I COULD CHANGE ANYTHING, IT WOULD BE...

_____

_____

_____

_____

_____

_____

_____

_____

_____

_____

_____

_____

_____

_____

_____

_____

_____

_____

5 PEOPLE I AM MOST GRATEFUL FOR

1. _____
2. _____
3. _____
4. _____
5. _____

5 THINGS I AM GRATEFUL FOR

1. _____
2. _____
3. _____
4. _____
5. _____

5 THINGS I WOULD LIKE TO DO

1. _____
2. _____
3. _____
4. _____
5. _____

SOMETHING I THOUGHT OF...   *Today is* _____

_____

_____

_____

Treasured Memories

USE THIS PAGE TO WRITE A POEM OR STORY

Today is _____

USE THIS PAGE TO WRITE A POEM, STORY OR DRAW HOW YOU FEEL

_____

_____

_____

_____

_____

_____

_____

_____

Treasured Memories

Here's a poem I wrote in memory of my brother
who I lost in 2008 and will always miss.

YOU ARE NOT HERE...
You are not here as you were before
I cannot see you anymore
Why did you have to go away?
I miss you every single day
I think about you all the time
I feel like you left me behind
They say you are a spirit who will always be with me
And that your soul is now worry-free
Will you watch me in life as I walk?
Will you be here when I need to talk?
I wonder if one day we will be together
One day would be better than never
I will keep your memory close to my heart
My love for you will never part

To Jamie,
Love, your sister

Some things to know...

Death is natural

Every living thing has a time to live and a time to die. This includes plants, insects, animals and people. When you lose someone you love, it hurts and it can take a long time to feel better about it. Everyone needs a different amount of time to heal. For some, it may be weeks or months, and for others, it may take years. There is no time limit, but one thing for certain is that it is never a good idea to hold in all of your feelings. My best advice is to talk to a parent, adult, trusted friend, school counselor, family member or therapist/counselor.

Healthy ways to cope with loss

- Share your feelings with others
- Allow yourself to experience sadness
- Write down your feelings
- Draw pictures
- Store notes, memorabilia and photos in a memory box
- Do things you enjoy
- Speak to members of our church
- Spend time with people you like and who treat you well
- Think about good times
- Pray
- Exercise
- Create art
- Plant a tree or memory a garden

SOME THINGS I THINK WILL HELP ME FEEL BETTER

_____

_____

_____

_____

_____

_____

_____

_____

_____

_____

_____

_____

_____

_____

_____

_____

_____

_____

I feel like writing...   *Today is* _____

_____

_____

_____

_____

_____

_____

_____

_____

_____

_____

_____

_____

_____

_____

_____

_____

_____

_____

I feel like writing...   *Today is* _____

_____

_____

_____

_____

_____

_____

_____

_____

_____

_____

_____

_____

_____

_____

_____

_____

_____

_____

_____

_____

I feel like writing...   *Today is* _____

_____

_____

_____

_____

_____

_____

_____

_____

_____

_____

_____

_____

_____

_____

_____

_____

_____

_____

I feel like writing...   *Today is* _____

_____

_____

_____

_____

_____

_____

_____

_____

_____

_____

_____

_____

_____

_____

_____

_____

_____

_____

_____

_____

I feel like writing...   *Today is* _____

_____

_____

_____

_____

_____

_____

_____

_____

_____

_____

_____

_____

_____

_____

_____

_____

_____

_____

I feel like writing...   *Today is* _____

_____
_____
_____
_____
_____
_____
_____
_____
_____
_____
_____
_____
_____
_____
_____
_____
_____
_____
_____
_____

I feel like writing...   *Today is* _____

_____

_____

_____

_____

_____

_____

_____

_____

_____

_____

_____

_____

_____

_____

_____

_____

_____

_____

_____

I feel like writing...   *Today is* _____

_____

_____

_____

_____

_____

_____

_____

_____

_____

_____

_____

_____

_____

_____

_____

_____

_____

_____

_____

The rest of the pages have been left blank for
you to write, draw, doodle or do as you wish!

Treasured Memories

Treasured Memories

Treasured Memories

Treasured Memories

Treasured Memories

Treasured Memories

Treasured Memories

www.ingramcontent.com/pod-product-compliance
Lightning Source LLC
LaVergne TN
LVHW021118080426
835509LV00021B/3438